HUMONGOUS FUNGUS

Written by **Lynne Boddy**
Illustrated by **Wenjia Tang**

DK

CONTENTS

DK | Penguin Random House

Written by Lynne Boddy
Illustrated by Wenjia Tang

Editor Kat Teece
Designer Bettina Myklebust Stovne
US Editor Mindy Fichter
US Senior Editor Shannon Beatty
Managing Editor Jonathan Melmoth
Managing Art Editor Diane Peyton Jones
Production Editor Dragana Puvacic
Production Controller Barbara Ossowska
Project Picture Researcher Sakshi Saluja
Creative Director Helen Senior
Publishing Director Sarah Larter

MIX
Paper | Supporting
responsible forestry
FSC™ C018179

This book was made with Forest Stewardship Council™ certified paper—one small step in DK's commitment to a sustainable future. For more information go to www.dk.com/our-green-pledge

A catalog record for this book is available from the Library of Congress. ISBN 978-0-7440-3333-5

DK books are available at special discounts when purchased in bulk for sales promotions, premiums, fund-raising, or educational use. For details, contact: DK Publishing Special Markets, 1745 Broadway, 20th Floor, New York, NY 10019 SpecialSales@dk.com

First American Edition, 2021
Published in the United States by DK Publishing
1745 Broadway, 20th Floor, New York, NY 10019

Copyright © 2021 Dorling Kindersley Limited
DK, a Division of Penguin Random House LLC
23 24 25 10 9 8 7
014–321128–Jul/2021

Printed and bound in China

www.dk.com

THE FUNGUS KINGDOM

The vast fungus kingdom has around four million species—or maybe even more. That's ten times more fungi than plants, and 600 times more fungi than mammals. Here are the main fungus types.

Mushrooms

These are the fruit bodies of some fungi. They make spores, which grow into new fungi. The body of the fungus is the mycelium, made of a network of threadlike structures, called hyphae.

Blue roundhead fungus

Hyphae

When we think of fungi we usually think of mushrooms, but there are many more types.

Yeasts

The bodies of some fungi are single cells, called yeasts. Some fungi can have bodies that are hyphae or yeasts. These can switch between yeasts or hyphae.

Aquatic fungi

Microscopic chytrid fungi live in wet places. Hyphae grow into plant or animal cells to feed. Their spores can swim to new food.

Plant cells are the tiny building blocks of plants.

Fungi look a little like plants, but they are more closely related to humans!

Black tulip fungus

The hyphae grow in the food.

Food surface

Clumps of pin mold spores look like black dots on bread or fruit.

Sac Fungi

Like mushroom fungi, the main body of a sac fungus is the mycelium. Some have fruit bodies, which are large enough to see without a microscope. These contain many eight-spore sacs.

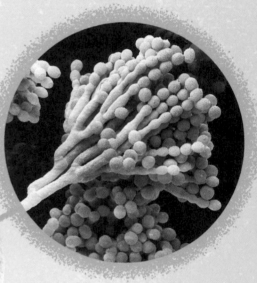

Some molds are sac fungi. They make chains of spores on the end of a hypha, instead of inside a fruit body.

Molds

Molds are a lot of different fungi that rot food and other things. Their hyphae make the surface they are rotting look fuzzy. There are a lot of spores on the ends of hyphae.

THE GREENING OF THE EARTH

The Earth's early landscapes were bare and rocky. The only plants were in water. Fungi helped plants move onto land, and to grow upward into the trees you see today.

Waterbound plants

At first, all life was in the water. Plants take in nutrients to keep them healthy, and the nutrients were dissolved in the water. On land, nutrients were in rock and young soil, and very hard to get.

Early land plants

500 million years ago tiny plants, such as mosses and liverworts, began to move onto land. But they had no roots to take in nutrients and water, so they teamed up with fungi...

fungus hyphae connected with early land plants.

Swapping food

Plants can make energy foods but fungi cannot. Fungi can absorb nutrients and water from soil, unlike many plants. So, the two link up and swap food, nutrients, and water.

Plants produce oxygen, which animals need to breathe to survive.

The plant gives the fungus sugars.

The fungus gives the plant water and nutrients from soil or rock.

Modern plants

Plants use sunlight energy to make sugars for food. Animals cannot make their own food, so they eat plants or other animals.

Without fungi

With fungi

Better together

All trees, and most other plants, still depend on fungal partners attached to their roots. Plants are animal food and keep our ecosystems thriving. Fungi keep plants going!

7

NATURE'S HELPERS

Without fungi, the ecosystems that thrive on land would not work. Fungi provide food for plants and animals, create places for them to live, and get rid of dead things.

Chicken of the woods

Insect homes

Wood rotted by fungi inside old trees is home to thousands of insects. Here, the creepy crawlies can eat the nutritious fungus.

Fly agaric

Common puffball

Animal food

The fruit bodies of fungi, such as mushrooms, are food for many animals. Insects eat hyphae too, and some even grow fungi for food.

Latticed stinkhorn

Plant food

Fungi feed most of our plants. Their hyphae grow into fine plant roots. They take up water and nutrients from the soil, and feed it to the roots.

Hyphae

The fungus grows inside the leaves.

Endophyte fungus

Plant protection

Fungi can live inside plant leaves and stems. Here, the fungus might kill germs, protect the plant from being eaten, or help it to grow.

Fungi are used to make medicine for humans.

Inside animals

Fungi live on the outside and inside of animals. Most help the animals stay healthy, though others cause them a lot of trouble!

Big cow fungus

Recycling

Fungi break down dead things, cleaning up the landscape and releasing the nutrients into the soil. Plants need these nutrients to survive.

A SPORE'S JOURNEY

A spore is the part of a fungus that grows into a new fungus. Many fungi make spores inside a fruit body, such as a mushroom. Others make chains of spores on the end of a hypha.

Making spores

Mushroom spores are made in the gills. Spores are shot off into the gap between the gills, or puff from puffballs. They then fall, and spread in the wind.

Spreading far and wide

Most mushroom spores are spread in the wind, but are dropped to the ground very close to the fruit body. A few may blow far away.

Gills

Cells in the gills make spores in groups of four.

Taxi

Spores of some fungi hitch a ride on flies or insects to travel away from the parent. The flies are attracted to the fungi by their tasty smell.

Some fungi produce over 30 billion spores a day!

Mold spores

If you zoomed in on a patch of mold, you'd spot tiny balloon-shaped sacs on the tips of spindly hyphae. Spores are made inside these sacs.

Every year, fungi release 110,231,131,092 lb (50,000,000,000 kg) of spores into the air.

Spotting spores

Spores come in different shapes. They are so small that they are hard to spot. But if there are a lot together, shot out by a puffball, the spores can look like a small cloud.

Growing

Conditions have to be perfect for a spore to germinate, or grow. The soil has to be warm and damp, with plenty of food. Most spores die, but a few will become a new mycelium.

Hyphae sprout from the spores.

Double protection

Spores are made on a mushroom's gills. *Amanita* mushrooms have a veil that protects the gills, and a second veil surrounding the whole fruit body.

Gills

Remains of gill veil

Veil

Remains of overall veil

GROWING MUSHROOMS

A mushroom is a little like the flower or fruit of a flowering plant. It is sometimes called a fruit body. Seeds are made in the fruits of plants, and spores are made in fungus fruit bodies.

Bigger and bigger

When the mushroom begins to form, a thin skin—the veil—joins the cap to the stem. The veil is a protective structure that keeps the mushroom's delicate parts intact as it pushes up through soil.

Joining forces

Before the fungus can make a fruit body, two parent mycelia need to join together. Enough food must have been saved, and certain weather is needed for the mushroom to grow.

Fly agaric fungus

When the veil breaks, a ring is left on the stalk and another is left at the base—called the volva. Little pieces of veil are left on the cap—the white flecks on the fly agaric.

Web cap fungus

The Cortinarius fungus' veil is a web of fine fibers (threads). Some of the web is left on the stalk when the veil breaks.

Remains of the veil can help you tell what type of mushroom it is.

Remains of veil

Veil

Many fungi only feed on dead things.

Parasol mushroom

This caterpillar was killed and eaten by a white muscardine fungus.

Some fungi kill animals.

HOW DOES A FUNGUS FEED?

Unlike plants, fungi cannot make sugars from carbon dioxide using sunlight energy. They need food that has already grown. The mycelium is the main part of the fungus. It finds and digests food.

feeding filaments

The mycelium is a network of fine, threadlike filaments, called hyphae. These are narrow, but together they have a big surface to soak up food molecules.

14

Fungus Food

Together, the kingdom of fungi can feed on everything that grows in nature. Different types might feed on simple food, such as sugars, on all or part of a plant or animal, or even on poop!

Some fungi swap food with other organisms.

Leafcutter ants take leaves to fungi growing in their nests as ant food.

Rust fungi are parasites that feed on living plants.

Some fungi kill plants.

Enzymes allow hyphae to bore into wood.

Enzymes are released.

Hyphae

Big food molecules are broken down.

Small molecules are absorbed.

There are fewer nutrients here.

External digestion

Humans eat food and digest it with enzymes in their gut. Fungi release enzymes to digest food outside of their bodies. They then soak it up.

There are a lot of nutrients here.

Sharing meals

Hyphae with a lot of nutrients can share them with hyphae that need them, through the network. The hyphae swap messages, too, such as "need food" or "food found, stop searching."

Forest-floor wars

If a battle is a draw, the fungi make a barrier around their territory, like a wall around a human home. Each of the lines we see in wood is a barrier around the space where a fungal individual is living.

FUNGUS WARS

Fungi rarely grow on their own, and when they meet a fungus of another species, they usually fight over nearby food. The loser dies and the winner gets the food, but sometimes it is a draw.

Mycelium battles

When fungi growing across soil meet, they produce chemicals to try to kill the other. They also make chemicals to defend themselves, if the other attacks.

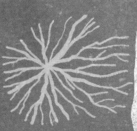

Neither fungus passes the battle zone.

Win, lose, or draw

Sometimes the battle is a draw, and a fungus keeps its own territory. Sometimes one fungus kills the other, and takes its space and food. To win, a fungus often changes what it looks like.

16

Piggyback fungi

Some fungi eat other fungi. They might form fruit bodies on the mushrooms on which they are feeding.

Powdery piggyback grows on the blackening brittlegill mushroom.

Parasitic bolete grows on earthball fungi.

Bonnet mold sometimes grows from the cap of a bonnet fungus.

Chemical warfare

Some fungi fight without touching. They poison the other fungus with gases or chemicals that move through whatever they are growing on.

Parasites

A parasite feeds off its host. Some parasitic fungi feed on the hyphae of others. They often coil tightly around the other fungus. Sometimes they grow into its hyphae.

Loser

Winner

The winner has changed what it looks like.

The hyphae of the parasite grow into the other fungus.

The parasitic fungus coils tightly around the other fungus' hyphae.

17

Witch's butter

Hairy curtain crust

Smokey bracket

Waxy crust

MUSHROOM FOREST

There are well over 30,000 types of mushroom fungi, which come in a forestful of shapes, sizes, and colors. Mushrooms can look like shelves (called brackets), balls, clubs, crusts, or jelly!

Porcelain fungus

Oyster mushroom

Shaggy scaly cap

Wrinkled crust

The most mushrooms can be seen in autumn.

Honey fungus

Sulphur tuft

Puffballs and earthstars

The spores are formed inside the fruit body. A hole forms at the top, and the spores are puffed out when it is nudged by a raindrop, twig, or animal.

Earthstar

Turkey tail

Oak mazegill

Common puffball

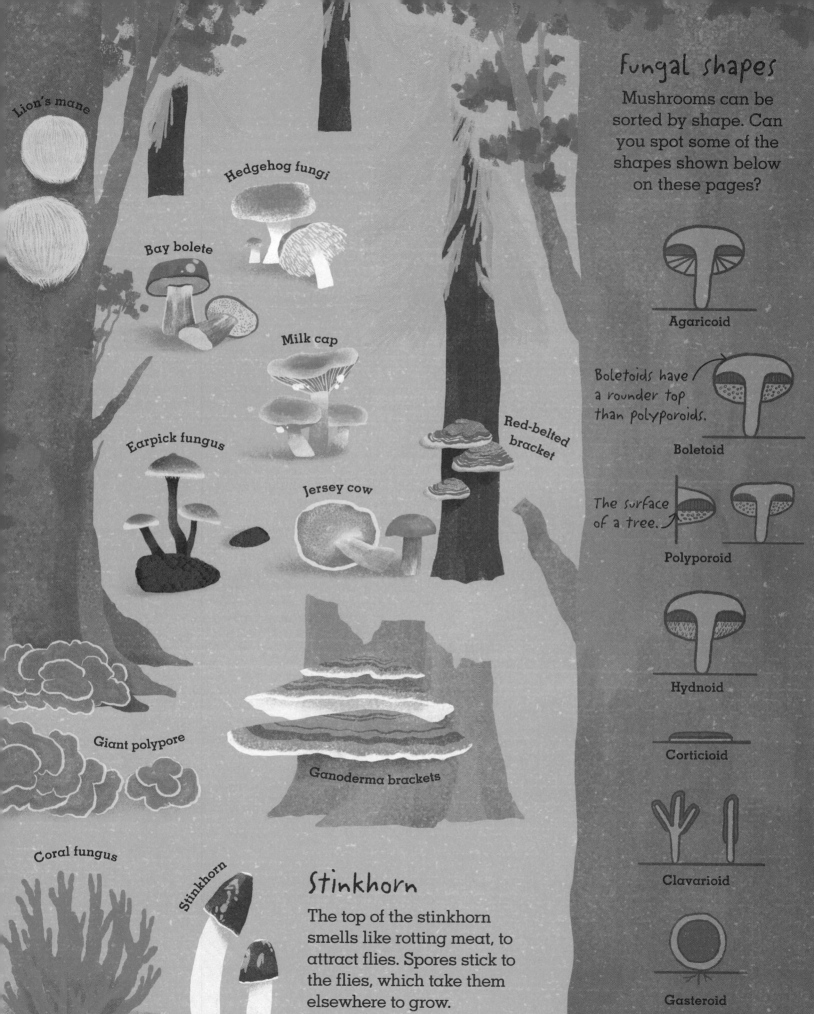

Lion's mane

Hedgehog fungi

Bay bolete

Milk cap

Earpick fungus

Jersey cow

Red-belted bracket

Giant polypore

Ganoderma brackets

Coral fungus

Stinkhorn

Stinkhorn

The top of the stinkhorn smells like rotting meat, to attract flies. Spores stick to the flies, which take them elsewhere to grow.

Fungal shapes

Mushrooms can be sorted by shape. Can you spot some of the shapes shown below on these pages?

Agaricoid

Boletoids have a rounder top than polyporoids.

Boletoid

The surface of a tree.

Polyporoid

Hydnoid

Corticioid

Clavarioid

Gasteroid

SAC FUNGI

These fungi come in all shapes and sizes, from microscopic to the size of a mushroom. Each contains many sacs of spores—usually eight spores in each sac.

The spore sacs are long and thin.

Morels

If you spot a fruit body that looks a little like a honeycomb, it could be a morel. Lots of saucers are joined together to form the honeycomb, which is raised off the ground by a stalk.

Cups and saucers

These fungi have spore sacs lining the upper side of their fruit body. Raindrops pick up spores when they splash from the cup, and carry them away.

King Alfred's cakes look
like lumps of coal.

The flasks grow
in layers, with
the newest on
the outside.

Truffles tend to grow below ground.

Spore sacs burst
or break down
to release spores.

Truffles

Truffles are like buried
treasure because some
species are sold for an
incredible amount of
money. Pigs love them,
and will lead truffle
hunters to the right spots.

Flasks

Some sac fungi make sacs in
fruit bodies shaped like flasks
(round bottles). Some flasks
are visible, while others
grow in the plant on which
the fungus is feeding.

21

Oyster mushroom

EDIBLE...

Fungi are food for insects and some mammals, including humans! They contain protein, which helps your muscles grow.

Some fungi are too tough to chew. Hundreds are edible but tasteless, or taste horrible!

Artist's conk

Chicken of the woods

Warning!

Poisonous fungi can look very similar to edible ones. NEVER risk eating fungi that grow in the wild.

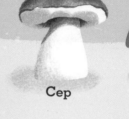

Cep

Weeping bolete

Common puffball

Puffballs contain masses of spores, which puff out when poked. Most puffballs are edible, but there are poisonous fungi that look very similar.

Chanterelle

Field mushroom

Common puffball

Greencracked brittlegill

This is often found under sweet chestnut trees, but also others. It is a partner with tree roots, feeding them with water and nutrients from the soil.

Horn of plenty

Greencracked brittlegill

Parasol mushroom

Saffron milk cap

22

OR POISONOUS

Although some fungi are safe to eat, others are very poisonous. Some fungi make you sick, and some will even kill you if you eat them.

Looks can lie

A fungus that could make you very sick may look just like an edible mushroom. Compare these fungi with their edible lookalikes on the opposite page. Can you tell the difference?

The death cap

Amanita phalloides is deadly poisonous. It is said that the ancient Roman emperor Claudius was killed by this fungus. He thought he was eating an edible species that looked almost the same.

A deadly fungus called web cap can be mistaken for cep.

The poisonous jack-o-lantern looks like chanterelle.

Young, poisonous amanitas can look like edible puffballs.

Fly agaric is poisonous to flies as well as people. People used it to poison flies in the past!

Insect food

Your body works in different ways than insects, so poisonous fungi might not harm them. Slugs and snails love some mushrooms that would make you sick.

23

FAIRYTALE FUNGI

Fungus fruit bodies often appear overnight. They can have strange shapes and bright colors, or form mysterious looking rings. In the past, people thought that these were signs of magic...

Grass killed by a fungus.

Dead grass

Rings of dead grass and bare earth can sometimes be spotted in grassland. These are formed by a fungus in the soil, killing the grass.

Feeding the grass

Rings of lush grass can also be formed by fungi. The grass is helped to grow by a fungus hidden in the soil.

The fungus feeds the grass roots and helps it grow.

Mushroom ring

The fungus mycelium grows outward from the center, year after year. The old parts in the middle eventually die, leaving the ring.

Tree ring

Sometimes a ring of fruit bodies can form around a tree. These fungi are attached to the tree's roots. Their hyphae feed water and nutrients to the tree.

Fungus rings can grow for hundreds of years, becoming wider and wider.

Strange looks

Fungi can look like magical substances or gruesome finds, such as human fingers! In the past, they were often named for their odd looks.

Witch's butter

Yellow brain fungus

Dead man's fingers

Devil's fingers

Folklore

Many stories have been made up about fungi. Once upon a time in the UK, people believed that fungus rings were caused by fairies dancing in a circle!

Fruticose lichen

Lichens come in many shapes and sizes. Fruticose lichens are bushy or dangle from branches.

Most lichens are sac fungi (see pages 20—21), with cup-shaped fruit bodies.

Foliose lichen

Foliose lichens are like a sandwich. The outside layers are a skin of tightly woven hyphae. Inside is a looser weave of hyphae. Algae cells are just below the upper skin.

Foliose lichens look like leaves, with different upper and lower surfaces.

Crustose lichen

These are crust-like lichens, completely attached to the things on which they grow. Like other lichens, they can live for a long time and grow very large.

LICHENS

Carpetlike or shrubby lichens, stuck to rocks and tree trunks, are actually fungi that have teamed up with algae or cyanobacteria. The fungus provides water and nutrients, while its partner feeds it carbohydrates.

Squamulose Lichen

These lichens have small, overlapping scales called squamules. The squamules break off to form new lichen patches.

A few lichens are mushroom fungi.

Reindeer lichen is the main diet of reindeer in winter.

Some lichens are thousands of years old.

Reindeer Lichen

This hardy lichen covers vast areas of often-freezing tundra and sub-arctic forest. It can be more than 6 in (15 cm) deep. Unlike most lichens, reindeer lichens can grow very quickly.

There are over 20,000 known species of lichens.

Desert Lichen

These lichens grow in the extreme climate of hot, dry deserts. Neither the fungi nor the algae could survive here on their own.

The bright colors of flowers attract insects that spread their pollen, which plants need to make seeds. But mushrooms don't have pollen to spread, so why do they come in many colors?

Blackening waxcap

Scarlet waxcap

Parrot waxcap

Golden waxcap

It's a mystery

Some scientists think colors could be a warning to animals not to eat poisonous mushrooms. For other fungi, color might protect them from harmful sunlight. There is still a lot to learn!

Indigo milk cap

Scientists do not know why many fungi are brightly colored.

Scarlet elf cup

Amethyst deceiver

Warning colors

The bright colors of some animals keep them safe. The color warns other animals not to try to eat them because they are poisonous—or pretending to be!

DARK...

Turkey tail

Helvella corium

Entoloma

Bird's nest

Keeping warm

Animals that live in cold places are often darkly colored. This is because dark colors absorb heat, so the animals warm up quicker. Fungi in colder places are darker too, for the same reason.

OR GLOWING

Attracting attention

More than 80 mushrooms glow a greenish color in the dark. Some scientists believe this attracts insects who spread spores, but no one knows for sure.

Glow-in-the-dark mushrooms and mycelium on tree trunks can make the tree look as though it is on fire!

Shining lichens

Lichens do not glow in the dark like some mushrooms. But if you shine ultraviolet light on them the colors can be amazing!

PLANT PARTNERS

All plants have partnerships with fungi. Tiny colonies of fungi live within leaves and stems. Fungi are often attached to roots too, making a network in the soil.

Wood-wide web

Each tree has a lot of fungus partners in the soil. They can be the same or different species. The mycelium can connect between roots on the same tree and on different trees.

The roots of trees form partnerships, called ectomycorrhizas. The hyphae grow in the soil and soak up water and nutrients.

Bluebell

Within the root cells, hyphae coil or branch out.

Growing into plants

The most common type of mycorrhiza (a partnership between a mycelium and plant roots) forms on the roots of non-woody plants. The fungus grows into the plant's cells and into the soil.

Dumpy fungus-roots

The fungus and tree join in short stumpy roots at the ends of larger roots. Hyphae cover the ends of roots, forming a fungus sock.

fungus net

Hyphae grow into the root and form a network. They get water and nutrients from soil, and pass these to the tree through the network. The tree gives the fungus sugars.

A teaspoon of soil can contain up to 6.2 miles (10 km) of hyphae!

Ghost pipe

Cheaters

A few species of plants do not have chlorophyll—a chemical needed to make make sugars. As well as water and nutrients, the fungi give these plants sugars, which they get from a tree.

Fungus hyphae can connect to cheater plants and to trees.

PLANT KILLERS

Although most fungi help to keep plants healthy, some kill their roots or leaves, or even the whole plant. They can kill garden flowers, food crops, and even tall trees.

Soybean rust

Patches of cells all over a soybean plant's leaves are killed by this fungus. The leaves fall off and fewer soybeans are made.

Panama disease

Inside banana plants, this fungus stops water moving from the roots to the leaves, so the plant wilts. Some people think it could wipe out banana crops!

Powdery mildew

Many different fungi cause mildew on plants. They form white powdery spots on leaves. The fungi take the plants' water and nutrients.

Corn smut

The fungus *Ustilago maydis* infects all parts of the corn plant. The corn kernels swell up, forming galls, which are a food called *huitlacoche* in Mexico.

Meal stealers

In total, the main fungus diseases of rice, wheat, soybean, corn, and potato cause losses that would have fed over a billion people.

Dutch elm disease

Landscapes can be altered by fungal diseases. Elm trees were once very common, but have almost disappeared because of Dutch elm disease.

The spores are carried on beetle bodies and enter the tree when beetles feed on its twigs.

Rice blast

This fungus grows into plant cells, which are killed after five days. In each dead area, thousands of spores are made, which can infect other plants.

Wheat stem rust

Rust fungi make reddish orange spores that look like rust. This fungus has to live on one plant species and then another to complete its life cycle.

Gray mold

Botrytis can infect over 200 plant species. It thrives in humid conditions. The fuzzy gray mold produces thousands of spores that spread the disease.

Potato late blight

Phytophthora infestans (similar to but not actually a fungus) kills potato plants and rots the tubers. It caused the Irish Potato Famine in the mid-1800s.

33

FUNGAL FOOD

Some of your favorite foods or drinks might not exist without fungi! They are used to create a lot of tasty things. Many types of mushrooms are delicious to eat all by themselves.

Field mushroom

Ear fungus

Lion's mane

Cauliflower mushroom

Cep

Tasty mushrooms

Edible fungi don't just have nice flavors—they are good for you, too! They contain a lot of proteins, which your body uses to build muscles. They also contain B vitamins, which keep you healthy.

Hidden chefs

Fungi are used to make a lot of different kinds of foods. Cheese is produced by adding a chemical called an enzyme to milk—and fungi make the enzyme! They are also responsible for tasty breads, sauces, drinks, and more...

Citric acid is made by a type of mold. The acid is added to canned fruit to stop the fruit from losing vitamin C, which helps keep you healthy. It also adds a sour flavour to sodas.

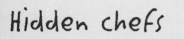

Aspergillus niger

Soy sauce

Canned fruit

Soda

Tempeh is made by growing Rhizopus fungus on soybeans.

Soy sauce is made by growing Aspergillus oryzae on mashed-up soybeans and wheat.

Tempeh

Cocoa beans

Chocolate is made from cocoa beans, but fresh beans are too bitter to eat! Fungi and bacteria rot the coating to make them tasty.

Camembert

Roquefort

Bread

Yeast fungi produce the gas carbon dioxide, which makes bread rise.

The texture, flavor, and smell of Camembert and Roquefort cheese are produced by types of Penicillium fungi.

ECO-FRIENDLY FUNGI

Plants make billions of pounds of new plant material every year. Most of this dies, and it would stick around if fungi didn't break it down—releasing the nutrients locked inside, which other plants eat.

White rot

Some fungi can use all of the chemicals in wood, so the wood becomes bleached. This is called white rot. The wood is gradually rotted away until it completely disappears.

Brown rot

Other fungi can use all of the chemicals in wood except lignin. These are called brown rot fungi, as the lignin they leave behind is a brown color.

Some fungi break down pollutants in soil and water, such as oil, which are harmful for wildlife.

Earpick fungus (Auriscalpium vulgare) rots pine cones.

Lanzia echinophila, a cup fungus, feeds on the outer spiny shells of sweet chestnuts.

The hat thrower

This breaks down animal dung. It shoots spores 3 ft (1 m) away from the dung, which stick to blades of grass. An animal eats the grass, and the fungus comes out in more dung, ready to rot it.

Kingdom fungi can break down all materials made by plants, animals, and microbes in nature.

Aspergillus tubingensis can break down plastic.

Plastic problem

Billions of tons of plastic are made every year, but it takes hundreds of years to break down—so waste is piling up. In 2017, a plastic-eating fungus was found that could help to solve this problem.

Horn stalkball

Some fungi specialize in breaking down hair or nail. The horn stalkball feeds on animal horns.

Different species of fungi feed on different things.

ANIMAL FRIENDS

Some animals team up with fungi to get help to digest the food they eat, or to protect themselves. In return, the animals take food to the fungi, or take the fungi to food.

Some termites make chimneys to cool the nest.

Neocallimastigomycota fungus

The termites eat balls of fungus.

Gut fungi

Some plant-eating mammals have several parts to their stomachs. In the first part, where there is little oxygen, fungi and microbes help digest food.

Termites

Some termites farm fungi to eat as food in their nests below ground. They bring plant material for the fungus to digest, and protect it from harmful microbes.

Holes are made when new adults fly out.

The wood wasp larvae and fungi can both damage the trees.

When the beetle eggs hatch, larvae also feed on the fungus.

The adult beetles feed on the fungi, and make sure that the fungi are not attacked by harmful microbes.

Fungi infect a few scale insects and feed on them.

Healthy scale insects are protected by layers of hyphae.

Wood wasps

Wood wasps carry *Amylostereum* fungi in pouches, and inject them into trees when they are laying their eggs. The fungi decay the wood, making it soft enough for the larvae (young insects) to eat and burrow through.

Beetle farmers

When ambrosia beetles fly to new trees, they take fungi with them. They inject eggs under the bark along with fungi, which grow in the tunnels the beetles make.

Scale insects

Scale insects feed by sucking sap from plants through a tube like a drinking straw. They are protected by *Septobasidium* fungus, but a few are fed on by the fungus.

Sea turtles

The fungus *Fusarium solani* kills masses of sea turtle eggs in their nests on beaches in the Atlantic, Indian, and Pacific Oceans. These animals are endangered, which means numbers are declining.

Some *Ophiocordyceps* fungi mummify their victims and later grow out as fruit bodies.

Insects

Some fungi kill insects and then feed on them. Insects can eat food crops, so some people use the fungi to get rid of these crop pests.

Bats

The little brown myotis hibernates in cold caves in eastern North America. The *Pseudogymnoascus destructans* fungus thrives in the caves, too, feeding on the live bats' skin. The bats wake up too often and run out of energy.

Humans spread fungal diseases

ANIMAL KILLERS

Fungi can be deadly. Some fungi kill animals for food. Insects and other small creatures often fall prey. Even some bigger animals can be killed.

Bees

The fungus *Nosema apis* infects the guts of bees. Many of the worker bees from a colony are killed, leaving only the queen and a few nurse bees.

Nematodes

Some fungi trap tiny nematode worms using sticky knobs or loops, or sticky or hooked spores. When the nematode has been trapped, the hyphae grow into its body to feed.

The white fungus can be seen on the bat's nose.

The fungus loop tightens to trap a nematode when it tries to wriggle through.

by trading things around the world.

Extinction

Fungi can wipe out entire species. *Batrachochytrium dendrobatidis* (BD for short) has caused the extinction of some animals, such as the golden toad in Costa Rica.

Controlling Flies

Chemicals in fruit bodies often attract insects. They help to spread spores. Sometimes, other chemicals stop flies from eating and laying eggs, so fruit bodies are not completely eaten.

Many mushrooms attract flies.

A "plug" of spores replaces the end of the cicada's body.

MUSHROOM MIND CONTROL

Confused cicadas

The *Massospora cicadina* fungus feeds on the end of a cicada's body. However, the fungus makes the cicada behave as if nothing has happened, so it can spread to other cicadas.

Spores get on the bodies of cicadas.

Some chemicals in mushrooms repel flies.

The ant dies and the fungus shoots out spores.

If you see an insect or animal behaving strangely, there might be a fungus to blame. Fungal chemicals can affect their behavior.

Zombie ants

Some zombie fungi need to get up high to spread their spores. The fungus growing in the ant makes it crawl up a plant and bite into it so it doesn't fall off.

Showers of spores infect ants.

Zombie fungi can't infect humans.

INSIDE US

Fungi are everywhere—even on your skin. Most of these won't cause you any harm. Other fungi live inside you, and spores floating in the air can be breathed in, making you sneeze.

Hay Fever

There are many more fungus spores in the air than pollen. If you are allergic to spores you might get hay fever when you breathe them in. This causes symptoms such as a runny nose.

Thrush

Candida yeast lives in your mouth, throat, and gut. There is usually a balanced amount alongside other microbes. Occasionally it can outgrow them and forms white patches.

Aspergillus fumigatus

Unlike most fungi, this can grow well at body temperature. We probably breathe in many of its spores every day, with no problem. Occasionally, people become ill with this fungus.

44

Ring worm

Ring worm is a red, itchy rash. It is actually not a worm at all, but a type of fungus called *Trichophyton*. It starts in the middle and grows outward in a circle.

Dandruff

The yeast *Malassezia* is the main cause of dandruff. It breaks down oils made by skin into chemicals that you may be sensitive to. The skin then sheds cells faster than normal.

Gut fungi

"Good bacteria" in your gut help with digestion and make vitamins. There are also fungi in your gut, but it's not yet known what they do.

Athlete's foot

Ever had an itchy feeling between your toes? It could be athlete's foot, but you don't need to be an athlete to get it. It is caused by another type of *Trichophyton* fungus.

MEDICINE MAKERS

Many of our most important medicines were discovered in fungi, and more will be discovered in the future. Even prehistoric humans used fungi as medicine—over 5,000 years ago!

Birch polypore

Penicillin was the first ever antibiotic—a medicine that kills bacteria.

Ötzi's fungus

Birch polypore was found in the belongings of Ötzi—a man whose body was frozen in ice in the Italian Alps, who lived 5,300 years ago! He probably ate the fungus to get rid of harmful nematode worms from his gut.

Penicillin

In 1928, Alexander Fleming was growing bacteria on plates of agar jelly. After a few weeks, he noticed that the *Penicillium* fungus had got in and was killing the bacteria around it. Bacteria cause some illnesses, and Alexander realized that penicillin was a cure.

Penicillium spores

Statins and steroids

Fungi make statins and steroids, which work as medicines in humans. Statins control cholesterol, which can be harmful in large amounts. Steroids treat illnesses including eczema, which affects skin.

New medicines

In search of new cures, scientists are looking at fungi used in traditional medicines, which some people have used for thousands of years. Reishi and turkey tail make chemicals that may treat diseases, but scientists need to research them properly.

Reishi

Turkey tail

Some people think lion's mane fungus has health benefits. However, do not pick it in the wild—it is an endangered species in some places.

Lion's mane

Helpful hormones

Fungi make chemicals called hormones. These can be used to make plants grow faster and produce more fruit, and to stop fruit falling off a plant too soon.

Biofuel power

Waste plant matter is made into sugars by fungi. These are then made into industrial alcohol by yeast fungi or bacteria. This can power cars!

AMAZING CHEMISTS

Fungi break down natural things into individual chemicals. They can make medicine and fuel, dispose of dangerous chemicals, and do much more besides—like little chemical factories.

Useful yeasts

Glycerol is made by yeasts, and can be used in all sorts of products. It is used as a sweetener and to make things such as soap, and antifreeze for car engines.

Quick chemists

Human chemists perform many chemical reactions in the laboratory to make medicines called steroids. A lot of these reactions can be done in a single step using a *Rhizopus* fungus.

Metal detecting

Fungi can extract metals from inside rock by releasing acids that break down the rock. Fungi can also recover metals from liquids and waste.

fungi can extract the tiny particles of gold sometimes found in water and lumps of iron.

Fungal Fashion

Fungi make enzymes used in the clothing industry. Enzymes are an ingredient in laundry detergent, they remove loose fibers (threads), and they are used to make stonewashed fabrics.

Stonewashed denim

Dye makers

Some colorful lichens and other fungi can be used to dye wool and silk. The fungus fruit body or lichen is soaked in hot water to get the dye.

49

HOME INVADERS

Fungi recycle dead things into nutrients that other living things can eat, but they sometimes start this job before we want them to! They can rot our food, belongings, and homes...

Eating moldy bread could make you unwell, so watch out for it!

In the kitchen

You need food for energy to keep you going and for nutrients to keep you healthy—but so do fungi! A mold fungus on food often looks like a furry patch.

Beneath the floor

The dry rot fungus eats wood in our roofs, ceilings, and floors. This makes the wood weaker and more likely to break. The fungus can spread from damp to dry areas, giving it the name "dry rot."

Dry rot spreads as rust-colored spores.

50

If homes are kept dry and airy, dry rot and mold are unlikely to grow.

On a shelf

Paper is made from a chemical called cellulose, which comes from plants. If paper is slightly damp, fungi can feed on the cellulose.

In the air

Mold spores travel through the air and find new things on which to grow. People who are allergic to the spores might feel poorly if they breathe them in.

Climbing the walls

Black mold can grow in damp places. It feeds on all sorts of materials, such as carpet, paint, paper, and glue. It makes a lot of spores and chemicals, which can be harmful if breathed in.

FLOATING FUNGI

Some fungi live in ponds, lakes, streams, rivers, and oceans. They are in the water, seaweed, living plants, dead plants, drifting wood, and in the mud at the bottom. Many are recyclers and partners with other organisms.

Strange spores

Spores of water fungi come in strange shapes—curves, coils, and tripods. This may help them to float, and to land on their tips on food. The tips make glue to stop the spores from being washed away.

Inside seaweed

Some fungi can kill plants and seaweed that grow in water. Seaweed has partner fungi inside them, which help them to grow. The fungi also protect very young seaweed from drying out.

Fungi break down dead things and release

Munching on mangroves

A wide range of fungi feed on mangroves, which are trees growing out of salty water. The fungi can be partners, killers, or rotters and important recyclers.

Hyphae

Chytrid spores

Tiny chytrids

Diatoms are tiny algae made of one cell, smaller than the width of a human hair. Hyphae of chytrid fungi can feed inside them. The chytrids form tiny sacs of swimming spores on the outside of the diatom.

A few fungi cause fish diseases.

Aspergillus sydowii bleaches (whitens), creates holes in, and kills sea fan corals.

Marine mysteries

Marine fungi are often overlooked by scientists, so we know little about them. Over a thousand species are known to live only in the sea, but there are likely 10,000 more still to be discovered.

nutrients in sediment.

HUMONGOUS FUNGUS

Most fungi are microscopic for most of the time.
But some grow gigantic mushroom fruit bodies.
A few form vast mycelia, which can weigh more
than a blue whale.

The main part of the fungus is hidden below ground.

Cords

Hyphae are tiny fungal filaments, which
are like threads. In some fungi, they can
grow together to form strands, or larger,
string-like structures called cords.

Gently turn over a
rotting log and often
you will find mycelium
cords growing from
the wood into the
soil beneath.

Cord networks

The cords form networks just
beneath the layer of leaves in a
forest. They link up rotting logs, fallen
branches, twigs, and other woody
material. The fungus can move water
and nutrients from one place to
another through the cords.

Rhizomorphs

These are often wider than cords with a thick, dark, waterproof coating. They are formed by honey fungi, called *Armillaria*. The rhizomorphs grow from tree to tree across the forest floor. A single individual fungus can form a huge network.

Giant fruit bodies

Termitomyces titanicus is a fungus whose mycelium is farmed by termites. It is said to be the largest edible fungus, sometimes with a mushroom cap of over 3 ft (1 m) across.

Giant puffballs can measure 60 in (150 cm) across.

Cep are usually the size of your hand.

The humongous fungus

In a vast forest in Oregon, an individual honey fungus rhizomorph network covers 3.5 miles² (9.5 km²) and weighs around 882,000 lb (400,000 kg). It is at least 2,500 years old, and is the largest organism in the world.

GLOBAL CHANGE

Our planet is changing. Humans are destroying habitats, and polluting air, land, and water with toxic chemicals and gases that affect the weather. These changes are causing problems for fungi.

Pollution

Gases made when we burn fossil fuels to power machinery and vehicles pollute the air, soil, and water. Chemicals used in factories and for farming pollute water and soil.

Ochre brittlegill

The blusher

Brown roll rim

Gray tooth

Devil's tooth

Changing fruiting

Fungi tend to grow in certain seasons, but the changing weather is confusing them. The autumn fruiting season is often longer, some fungi fruit earlier, and plant partners sometimes fruit later.

Vanishing fungi

Extra nitrogen is added to soil when fossil fuels are burned, and in farming to help plants grow. This has caused some plant-partner fungi to be lost.

Fungi are changing where they grow and when they fruit.

Earth is around 1.8 °F (1 °C) warmer than it was in 1900.

Changing use of land

Humans chop down trees for materials and to clear land for farming. They also cover land with buildings and roads. This destroys habitats for fungi.

By protecting habitats, humans can help fungi.

Spring fungi

Some fungi have always made fruit bodies in spring, but now many more do. This is because winters are warmer, so fungi can get food then, too.

Tree swapping

Some fungi grow on different trees than in the past. The ear fungus used to grow mostly on elder. It now grows on many trees—but mostly on beech.

Death cap is invasive throughout California.

Keep out

Fungi can get to places they did not live before and become invasive. This means they get rid of some native fungi, by fighting them or competing for food.

Wood-rotting sulphur tuft now fruits earlier in autumn than it used to, and even in spring.

SAVING THE FUTURE

Humans are causing the extinction of many plant, animal, and fungal species. Without fungi, the natural ecosystems of our planet would not work. Here's how you can protect fungi.

Don't pick them

In the high grasslands of the Himalayas, the caterpillar fungus has become endangered because some people believe it is a medicine and pick it. If you see a wild fungus, don't pick it (it could be poisonous, too).

Europe has lost most of its flower-rich hay meadows.

Be more natural

Fields for animals are now planted with a few fast-growing grasses, and fertilizers are added to help them grow. Fungi need soil with a lot of different plants and no fertilizers—so natural grasslands should be saved.

Earth tongue

Wax cap

Leave dead wood

Some rare fungi need big, old trees and logs, which take a long time to rot away. We must leave fallen trunks and dead branches in forests.

A fallen branch in a forest is a fungus' precious food.

Protect ancient trees

Fungi rotting the center of old trees is a natural part of the tree's life. It creates a habitat for insects, small mammals, and birds. We must not chop down ancient, hollowing trees.

GLOSSARY

Bracket

Shelf-shaped fruit body, often with tiny holes on the underside

Cap

Wide, top part of a mushroom fruit body, which sits on top of a stalk

Cell

Tiny building block of an organism

Cord

Visible, stringlike structure formed from hyphae

Cup

Fruit body shaped like a cup or saucer, with spores that are made in a lot of long, thin sacs on the inner surface of the cup

Cyanobacteria

Single-celled organisms that can make sugars from carbon dioxide using energy from sunlight

Earthstar

Fruit body similar to a puffball, but raised above the ground on stilts

Endophyte

Fungus that lives within a plant without harming it

Filament

Very fine, threadlike structure

Fruit body

Part of the fungus that makes spores, such as a mushroom or cup

Germination

When a hypha grows from a spore

Gill

Part of the mushroom, on the underside of the cap, where spores are made

Hypha

Microscopic filament (threadlike structure). A network of hyphae makes up the mycelium

Lichen

Fungus that partners up with algae or cyanobacteria

Mold

Fungus that does not produce large fruit bodies. The mycelium or spores are often green, blue, or black

Mushroom

Fruit body with a cap, gills, and stalk. The word is also used for fungi that make other types of fruit bodies, such as brackets, puffballs, and earthstars

Mycelium

Main body of most fungi, formed from a branching network of hyphae

Mycorrhiza

Partnership between a fungus mycelium and plant roots, in which food is swapped between the two

Nutrient

Chemical that organisms eat in order to grow and stay healthy

Organism

Living thing, such as a fungus, animal, or plant

Parasite

Organism that grows on or in another living organism, taking food out of it and giving nothing in return

Pollution

When harmful substances make their way into the air, soil, or a body of water

Puffball

Ball-shaped or pear-shaped fruit body, with spores that puff out of the top when the puffball is tapped

Rhizomorph

Visible, stringlike structure formed from hyphae, similar to but often wider than cords

Spore

Tiny cell produced by one or two parent fungi, which is carried away by the air or on an animal, and may grow into a new fungus

Stalk

Upright, cylindrical part of a mushroom, which raises the cap above the ground and connects it to the mycelium

Truffle

Underground fruit body

Yeast

Single-celled fungus

INDEX

ACKNOWLEDGMENTS

DK would like to thank: Vagisha Pushp for picture research; Vikram Singh for his design help; Polly Goodman for proofreading the book; and Helen Peters for the index.

The publisher would like to thank the following for their kind permission to reproduce their photographs:

(Key: a-above; b-below/bottom; c-center; f-far; l-left; r-right; t-top)

4 Alamy Stock Photo: Mediscan (br). **Dreamstime. com:** Alexander Kurlovich (ca). **5 Dreamstime. com:** Katyspichal (c). **Science Photo Library:** Power And Syred (cr). **8 Alamy Stock Photo:** Arterra Picture Library / Clement Philippe (cra). **9 Dreamstime.com:** Serban Enache (br). **Dr. Gareth Wyn Griffith:** (clb). **Dr. Yu-Ling Huang:** (ca). **10 Getty Images:** Stone / Ed Reschke (bc). **13 Dreamstime. com:** Alexander Potapov (cra). **14 Dreamstime.com:** Darius Baužys (tl). **Getty Images / iStock:** hsvrs (tr). **15 Alamy Stock Photo:** Redmond Durrell (tr). **21 Alamy Stock Photo:** Sabena Jane Blackbird (cla). **22 Dreamstime.com:** Aleksandar Milutinovic (bl); Richard Thomas (crb). **23 123RF.com:** Andrzej Tokarski / ajt (crb). **Alamy Stock Photo:** Imagebroker / Arco / O. Diez (ca). **Dreamstime.com:** Empire331 (clb, cra). **25 Getty Images / iStock:** gurkoao (br). **26 Alamy Stock Photo:** Sabena Jane Blackbird (cra). **27 Dreamstime.com:** Iakov Filimonov (ca). **28 Alamy Stock Photo:** Richard Becker (cla); Pat Canova (cr); Chris Mellor (br). **Dreamstime.com:** Werner Meidinger (ca); Whiskybottle (cra); Michaelimages (fcra). **Getty Images / iStock:** Azureus70 (bl); empire331 (cl). **29 Alamy Stock Photo:** Daniel Borzynski (bl); Bob Gibbons (cla). **Getty Images / iStock:** hekakoskinen (cb). **Getty Images:** Moment / Louise

Docker Sydney Australia (cr). **32 Alamy Stock Photo:** David Bleeker Photography (br). **33 Alamy Stock Photo:** Rosey. (tl); Thomas Weightman (br). **Dreamstime.com:** Floriankittemann (bl). **35 Nick Read:** (tc). **Science Photo Library:** Power And Syred (bl). **36 Dreamstime.com:** Matauw (c). **36-37 Dreamstime.com:** Alfio Scisetti / Scisettialfio (c). **37 Alamy Stock Photo:** Witold Krasowski (cb). **Dreamstime.com:** Muriel Lasure (ca). **Science Photo Library:** Wim Van Egmond (tc). **38 Dreamstime.com:** Apisit Wilaijit (c). **39 Alamy Stock Photo:** Richard Becker (cla); blickwinkel / F. Hecker (c). **40 Alamy Stock Photo:** Anton Sorokin (tc). **Dreamstime. com:** Heather Snow (c). **41 Dreamstime.com:** Somchai Khunwiset (c). **44 Alamy Stock Photo:** Icom Images (bc); **Dreamstime.com:** Dalius Baranauskas (cl). **45 Alamy Stock Photo:** Mediscan (tl); **Dreamstime.com:** Vchalup (cr); **Science Photo Library:** Dr P. Marazzi (cb). **46 Science Photo Library:** Biophoto Associates (crb). **47 Dreamstime. com:** Empire331 (bl). **Getty Images / iStock:** AnniePunyakorn (br); Krungchingpixs (c). **48 Dreamstime.com:** GCapture (ca); Anton Ignatenco (cla); Kingjon (br). **49 Dreamstime. com:** Anton Starikov (cb); Taigis (bc). **Getty Images / iStock:** Vaitekune (crb). **51 Science Photo Library:** Dr. Richard Kessel & Dr. Gene Shih, Visuals Unlimited (c). **52-53 Dreamstime.com:** Seadam. **53 Dreamstime.com:** Jdazuelos (crb). **55 Humongous Dreamstime.com:** Lightboxx (cl). **58 Dreamstime.com:** Jm73 (br, fbr). **59 123RF.com:** Eric Isselee / isselee (bl). **Dreamstime.com:** David Hansche (cb, crb); Henrikhl (tc)

All other images © Dorling Kindersley